This book belongs to:

_____

Christmas is drawing near, a time filled with magic, warmth, and joyful moments with loved ones. As we prepare to dive into this festive season, here's a playful twist to spark laughter and delightful conversations. Presenting 'Would You Rather: Christmas Edition for Kids'. Dive into these whimsical questions and discover a world of festive wonders. Perfect for family gatherings, school parties, or simply to share a chuckle with friends. Let the festive fun begin!

Would you rather ride on
Santa's sleigh
or
one of his reindeer?

Would you rather get a kiss
under the mistletoe from a
snowman
or
a reindeer?

Would you rather eat only candy canes

or

only gingerbread cookies for a week?

Would you rather have a snowball fight with elves

or

snowmen?

Would you rather wear ugly
Christmas sweaters every day
or
Christmas tree ornaments as
earrings?

Would you rather have every
day be Christmas
or
only once every ten years?

Would you rather sing carols with the Grinch

or

Frosty the Snowman?

Would you rather unwrap presents slowly

or

all at once like a tornado?

Would you rather decorate a 10-foot tall Christmas tree
or
a 10-foot wide gingerbread house?

Would you rather spend Christmas at the North Pole
or
on a tropical beach with Santa in shorts?

Would you rather have a red
Rudolph nose
or
elf ears for Christmas?

Would you rather give presents
or
receive presents?

Would you rather eat Christmas
dinner with Jack Frost
or
with Olaf from "Frozen"?

Would you rather have candy cane
fingers
or
snowball toes?

Would you rather have your Christmas tree lights always twinkling
or
playing Christmas jingles?

Would you rather have a white Christmas every year
or
a Christmas rainbow?

Would you rather be best friends
with an elf
or
a reindeer?

Would you rather be wrapped in
gift wrap
or
tangled in Christmas lights?

Would you rather have jingle bells
on your shoes
or
mistletoe on your hat?

Would you rather be one of
Santa's elves
or
one of his reindeer?

Would you rather get coal
or
broccoli in your stocking?

Would you rather eat a turkey-
sized candy cane
or
a candy cane-sized turkey?

Would you rather have a snow globe that shows your future

or

one that takes you to the past?

Would you rather have icicle fingers

or

snowflake eyelashes?

Would you rather drink hot cocoa
that's a bit too hot
or
a bit too cold?

Would you rather be a character
in "The Nutcracker"
or
"A Christmas Carol"?

Would you rather have Christmas
every day
or
once every 4 years like the
Olympics?

Would you rather slide down your
roof like Santa
or
climb up the chimney?

Would you rather play hide and
seek in a giant gingerbread house
or
in a huge pile of presents?

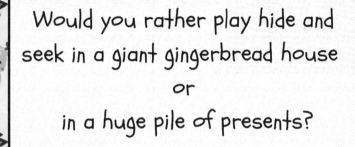

Would you rather be serenaded by
a choir of elves
or
by a solo singing snowman?

Would you rather help Mrs. Claus
bake cookies
or
help the elves make toys?

Would you rather have a pet
penguin
or
a pet polar bear for Christmas?

Would you rather have Christmas
trees for arms
or
snow globes for eyes?

Would you rather bring
snowmen to life
or
have Christmas trees talk?

Would you rather get letters from
all the toys you've received

or

from all the cookies you've eaten?

Would you rather dance with
sugarplum fairies

or

play games with Santa's elves?

Would you rather wear a beard like Santa's
or
a hat like Frosty's?

Would you rather live in a gingerbread mansion
or
a candy cane castle?

Would you rather use
marshmallows as pillows
or
candy canes as walking sticks?

Would you rather have stockings
for feet
or
ornaments for ears?

Would you rather pull Santa's sleigh
or
have Santa carry you around the world?

Would you rather have your house wrapped in gift wrap
or
covered in snowflakes?

Would you rather be gifted a
magic snowball
or
a magic ornament?

Would you rather speak only in
Christmas carol lyrics
or
only in reindeer sounds?

Would you rather have snow
always falling around you
or
have a personal choir singing
carols?

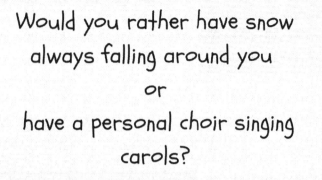

Would you rather be the star on
top of the Christmas tree
or
a present under it?

Would you rather make snow
angels
or
snowmen all day?

Would you rather always smell
like pine trees
or
cinnamon?

Would you rather jump into a pool of eggnog
or
a pool of melted chocolate?

Would you rather be the best gift wrapper in the world
or
the fastest Christmas tree decorator?

Would you rather have a nose that lights up like Rudolph's

or

have mistletoe growing from your hair?

Would you rather only be able to watch Christmas movies

or

listen to Christmas songs?

Would you rather have a snow globe stomach
or
candy cane bones?

Would you rather be friends with the Grinch before
or
after his change of heart?

Would you rather see Santa
or
his elves when you stay up on
Christmas Eve?

Would you rather throw a
Christmas party for toys
or
for snowmen?

Would you rather have Christmas
crackers explode with laughter
or
with joy?

Would you rather wear candy cane
glasses
or
have tinsel for hair?

Would you rather listen to a
reindeer's story
or
an elf's tale?

Would you rather have a sleigh
for a bed
or
ornaments for pillows?

Would you rather eat dinner with the characters from "Home Alone"
or
"The Polar Express"?

Would you rather have cookies
or
milk for hands?

Would you rather get stuck up a
chimney with Santa
or
get lost in the North Pole with
Rudolph?

Would you rather be greeted by
caroling mice
or
dancing presents every morning?

Would you rather spend a day in
Santa's workshop
or
in his candy kitchen?

Would you rather give gifts using
magic
or
receive gifts from magical
creatures?

Would you rather have
gingerbread teeth
or
candy cane nails?

Would you rather have a
snowstorm inside your house
or
turn your home into a giant
gingerbread house?

Would you rather make toys
or
test toys with the elves?

Would you rather spend Christmas
underwater with mermaids
or
in the sky with stars?

Would you rather turn snow into
chocolate
or
rain into candy?

Would you rather hug a
snowman
or
a reindeer?

Would you rather have the
voice of an angel
or
the baking skills of Mrs. Claus?

Would you rather fly around the
world delivering gifts
or
welcoming kids to the North
Pole?

Would you rather have a sleigh
bell ring every time you laugh
or
have snow fall every time you
sneeze?

Would you rather dance with
gingerbread men
or
sing with candy canes?

Would you rather wear mittens
all year round

or

a Santa hat?

Would you rather go ice skating
with elves

or

tobogganing with reindeer?

Would you rather be tiny like an elf

or

tall like a Christmas tree?

Would you rather have your room decorated by mischievous elves

or

helpful snowmen?

Would you rather wrap every
single present in the world
or
deliver them all in one night?

Would you rather have the ability
to turn anything into chocolate
or
have snowflakes that taste like
sugar?

Would you rather have a
Christmas tree that changes
colors
or
ornaments that tell stories?

Would you rather eat a giant
marshmallow snowman
or
a life-sized gingerbread house?

Would you rather go caroling
with animals
or
have a snowball fight against
them?

Would you rather have a talking
Christmas stocking
or
a dancing Christmas pudding?

Would you rather wake up as a
toy in Santa's bag
or
as a cookie in Mrs. Claus' kitchen?

Would you rather have a winter
wonderland in your backyard
or
a secret portal to the North
Pole in your closet?

Would you rather turn into a toy
on Christmas Eve
or
be able to bring toys to life?

Would you rather have the power
to make it snow
or
the power to light up houses
with festive cheer?

Would you rather spend a day
making snow angels
or
building a snow fortress?

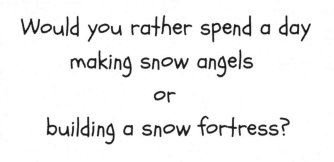

Would you rather celebrate
Christmas with the characters
from "Frozen"
or
from "The Nightmare Before
Christmas"?

Would you rather have a bath in
hot cocoa
or
a shower in candy cane
sprinkles?

Would you rather have all your
clothes made of wrapping paper
or
all your shoes made of
gingerbread?

Would you rather have reindeer antlers

or

a snowman's carrot nose?

Would you rather live in a world where Christmas trees walked

or

where snowmen talked?

Would you rather have your Christmas presents delivered by flying penguins

or

roller-skating polar bears?

Would you rather see the world from atop the highest Christmas tree

or

from inside the shiniest ornament?

Would you rather fight off a
snowman invasion
or
save Christmas from being stolen
by mischievous creatures?

Would you rather have tinsel
for hair
or
baubles for eyes?

Would you rather have the
strength of ten Grinches
or
the speed of ten reindeer?

Would you rather join a
snowman army
or
a gingerbread cookie militia?

Would you rather listen to the same Christmas song forever

or

never hear a Christmas song again?

Would you rather be a detective solving the mystery of Santa's missing sleigh

or

be on a quest to find the lost star of Bethlehem?

Would you rather be Santa's chief gift wrapper

or

his main cookie taste tester?

Would you rather be snowed in with Santa's elves

or

with characters from Christmas stories?

Would you rather wear shoes
that jingle
or
clothes that sparkle?

Would you rather get stuck in a
snow globe
or
inside a Christmas card?

Would you rather make toys
using magic
or
bake treats with fairy dust?

Would you rather fly with
Santa's reindeer
or
dance on the clouds with snow
fairies?

Would you rather build the biggest snowman ever

or

create the most magical snow scene?

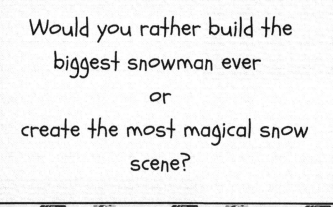

Would you rather have a pet snowman that melts every night and reforms every morning

or

a pet reindeer that can only fly on Christmas Eve?

Would you rather have a holiday dinner with Santa and Mrs. Claus

or

a festive tea party with the snow queen?

Would you rather have all your Christmas gifts be surprises

or

choose each one yourself?

Would you rather have every day
be Christmas for a year
or
have a super spectacular
Christmas once every 5 years?

Would you rather go on a sleigh
ride with Santa
or
a train ride on the Polar
Express?

Would you rather be able to
whisper to Christmas trees
or
sing duets with Christmas bells?

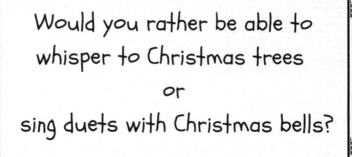

Would you rather create the
most beautiful ice sculptures
or
the most enchanting snow
scenes?

Would you rather be visited by
three Christmas ghosts
or
join Santa on his worldwide
delivery trip?

Would you rather lead the
Christmas parade
or
light up the town's Christmas
tree?

Would you rather have a
Christmas tree that grows candy
or
one that showers small gifts?

Would you rather celebrate
Christmas on the moon with
aliens
or
deep under the sea with
mermaids?

Would you rather bring joy to one
sad child on Christmas
or
give small gifts to a hundred
children?

Would you rather spend
Christmas in a gingerbread village
or
a candy cane forest?

Would you rather be able to turn anything into a Christmas ornament

or

bring any Christmas decoration to life?

Would you rather play in a band with Santa and his reindeer

or

be the lead in a Christmas play with elves?

Would you rather have
Christmas cookies magically
appear whenever you're hungry
or
have a cup of hot cocoa refill
itself?

Would you rather ride a
Christmas carousel with festive
creatures
or
slide down a giant candy cane?

Would you rather have a snowman
best friend who never melts
or
a reindeer buddy who visits every
Christmas?

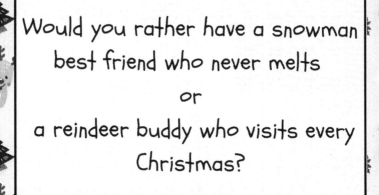

Would you rather spend a
day inside your favorite
Christmas ornament
or
take a trip inside a magical
snow globe?

Would you rather sleep in a bed
made of marshmallows
or
live in a house made of
gingerbread?

Would you rather be able to light
up like a Christmas tree
or
spread festive scents like cinnamon
and pine wherever you go?

Would you rather have a personal choir of elves singing your favorite tunes

or

a band of snowmen playing festive melodies?

Would you rather find a hidden Christmas village in the woods

or

discover a secret winter wonderland beneath your city?

Would you rather dance in the
Nutcracker ballet
or
sing solo in a Christmas concert?

Would you rather watch every
Christmas movie in one day
or
read all Christmas stories in
one night?

Would you rather celebrate
Christmas with fairy tale
characters
or
with superheroes wearing
festive costumes?

Would you rather unwrap a gift
that grants wishes
or
one that tells the future?

Would you rather have a Christmas sweater that's always warm and cozy

or

one that displays your favorite festive scenes?

Would you rather be given the ability to spread snow wherever you go

or

the power to make every day feel like Christmas?

Would you rather have an endless
supply of mistletoe

or

an everlasting Christmas wreath?

Would you rather have magical
Christmas stockings that fill
with surprises

or

a Santa hat that grants wishes
when worn?

Would you rather find the end of a rainbow during Christmas

or

see a constellation shaped like a Christmas tree?

Would you rather eat a five-course meal with the Snow Queen

or

have a cookie feast with gingerbread people?

Would you rather leave out
cookies for Santa
or
carrots for his reindeer?

Would you rather get a visit
from Jack Frost
or
the Sandman on Christmas Eve?

Would you rather celebrate
Christmas on a snowy mountain
top
or
on a sunny beach with sandmen
instead of snowmen?

Would you rather have a
snowball fight with Yetis
or
go ice fishing with talking
penguins?

Would you rather sing the longest
Christmas carol

or

play the biggest jingle bell?

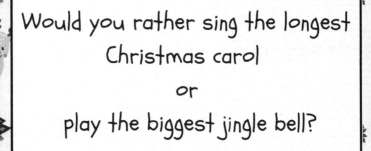

Would you rather have a
Christmas tree that can change
its theme with a thought

or

have ornaments that replay
your favorite memories?

Would you rather get a letter
from Santa every month
or
a call from an elf every week?

Would you rather be able to
decorate anything with a snap of
your fingers
or
make any dish taste like
Christmas?

Would you rather have the North Star guide you whenever you're lost

or

be able to call reindeer to your side whenever needed?

Would you rather be a Christmas detective solving festive mysteries

or

a Christmas superhero saving holidays?

Would you rather jump from one
Christmas cloud to another
or
surf on Northern Lights?

Would you rather be able to
whisper wishes to Santa's elves
or
listen to stories from Christmas
stars?

Would you rather be in charge of
painting the Northern Lights
or
choosing the color of each
snowflake?

Would you rather bake with
Mrs. Claus
or
build toys with the chief elf?

Would you rather be the guardian of a magical Christmas crystal
or
the keeper of Santa's secret map?

Would you rather decorate every home with Christmas magic
or
ensure every child receives a special festive storybook?

Would you rather experience
Christmas in slow motion
or
have the ability to revisit past
Christmases?

Would you rather go on a sleigh
ride around the world
or
explore hidden realms with Santa's
magic key?

Would you rather be able to
turn any grinchy mood festive
or
ensure that no Christmas tree
ever drops its needles?

Would you rather fill the world
with snowmen that dance at night
or
reindeer that create stars with
their hooves?

Would you rather have the gift of making everyone's Christmas wishes come true

or

be able to bring peace to any conflict during the holiday season?

Would you rather unwrap a gift that teleports you to the North Pole

or

one that allows you to understand animals during Christmas?

Would you rather organize a festive parade for magical creatures

or

a Christmas concert for mythical beings?

Would you rather have snowflakes that play melodies when caught

or

icicles that light up with rainbow colors?

Would you rather have your own personal snow cloud to bring winter joy
or
a magical Christmas bell to summon festive surprises?

Would you rather bring joy to a forgotten land with Santa
or
discover a new festive tradition with his elves?

Would you rather create the most
magical Christmas light display
or
write the most heartwarming
Christmas song?

Would you rather be the
person who decides the color of
Santa's new suit
or
the design of his next sleigh?

Would you rather be able to grant someone a white Christmas with a snap

or

ensure a cozy fireplace for everyone?

Would you rather be a Christmas astronaut discovering festive wonders in space

or

a Christmas explorer finding magical islands?

Would you rather have a Christmas tree that grows all year

or

a fireplace that tells festive tales?

Would you rather experience Christmas as one of Santa's reindeer

or

as a mischievous elf?

Would you rather be able to make every Christmas gift wrap itself
or
have every Christmas dinner cook to perfection on its own

Would you rather have candy canes grow in your garden
or
find festive golden coins under your pillow every morning?

Would you rather taste the first
snowflake of winter
or
catch the last star of Christmas
night?

Would you rather play hide and
seek in Santa's toy factory
or
have a snowball fight in his winter
garden

Would you rather design a new toy for Santa's workshop
or
come up with a new flavor for Mrs. Claus's cookies?

Would you rather ride a Christmas roller coaster made of candy canes
or
sail a river of melted snow chocolate?

Would you rather experience
Christmas from the perspective
of an ornament
or
from the point of view of a gift
under the tree?

Would you rather have the
power to fill stockings with
endless surprises
or
ensure that every Christmas
morning is sunny and bright?

Would you rather be known for telling the most captivating Christmas stories

or

for singing the most touching carols?

Would you rather have a pet polar bear that helps decorate your home

or

a team of penguins that wrap presents for you?

Would you rather spend a Christmas in a castle made of snow

or

in a palace made of twinkling lights?

Would you rather witness the magical birth of the first Christmas tree

or

be present when the first snowflake ever fell?

Would you rather be able to transform any object into a Christmas gift

or

turn any sad moment into a festive joy?

Would you rather see a Christmas rainbow after every winter shower

or

have festive fireworks every Christmas Eve?

Would you rather be greeted by singing snowflakes every morning

or

by dancing icicles every night?

Would you rather play festive pranks with Jack Frost

or

go on a Christmas adventure with the Snow Queen?

Would you rather have the ability to turn into a Christmas ornament at will

or

transform into a festive star?

Would you rather spend Christmas Eve at a ball with all festive characters

or

have a sleepover at Santa's workshop?

Would you rather have your thoughts broadcasted as Christmas jingles
or
have your moods reflected by changing Christmas lights?

Would you rather create snow with a wave of your hand
or
summon a festive breeze filled with the scent of Christmas?

Would you rather have a secret drawer filled with never-ending Christmas treats

or

a magical window showcasing festive scenes from around the world?

Would you rather have the skills to craft the most intricate snowflakes

or

the talent to mold the most lifelike snow sculptures?

Would you rather be the guardian of the enchanted Christmas book that holds all holiday secrets

or

the protector of the magical key that opens every festive door?

Would you rather have feet that squeak every time you walk

or

have hair that changes color every time you sneeze?

Printed in Great Britain
by Amazon